Rainforests

Maria Koran

EYEDISCOVER

EYEDISCOVER

Go to **www.eyediscover.com** and enter this book's unique code.

BOOK CODE

AVW42666

EYEDISCOVER brings you optic readalongs that support active learning.

Published by AV^2 by Weigl
350 5th Avenue, 59th Floor New York, NY 10118
Website: www.eyediscover.com

Library of Congress Control Number: 2019945849

ISBN 978-1-7911-0752-9 (hardcover)

Printed in Guangzhou, China
1 2 3 4 5 6 7 8 9 0 23 22 21 20 19

072019
121818

Project Coordinator: John Willis
Designer: Mandy Christiansen and Ana María Vidal

Weigl acknowledges Getty Images and iStock as the primary image suppliers for this title.

EYEDISCOVER provides enriched content, optimized for tablet use, that supplements and complements this book. EYEDISCOVER books strive to create inspired learning and engage young minds in a total learning experience.

Your EYEDISCOVER Optic Readalongs come alive with...

Audio
Listen to the entire book read aloud.

Video
High resolution videos turn each spread into an optic readalong.

OPTIMIZED FOR

- ✓ TABLETS
- ✓ WHITEBOARDS
- ✓ COMPUTERS
- ✓ AND MUCH MORE!

Rainforests

In this book, you will learn about

- what they are
- where they are
- what lives there

and much more!

Rainforests are large forests that get lots of rain.

6

Most rainforests are warm. They are known as tropical rainforests.

The Amazon rainforest is the largest rainforest. It is called the "lungs of the Earth" because it makes so much air safe to breathe.

About half of the world's plants and animals live in rainforests.

Rainforests are home to some of the most colorful frogs in the world.

Many kinds of birds live in the rainforest. Macaws are known for their different colors.

Orangutans are found in rainforests in Asia. They spend most of their lives in trees.

The rainforests are getting smaller. Every second, a forest the size of a football field is cut down.

Most of the world's plants and animals need rainforests to survive. It is important to keep rainforests safe.

RAINFORESTS BY THE NUMBERS

The **Amazon Rainforest** covers about **2,300,000** square miles. (6,000,000 square kilometers)

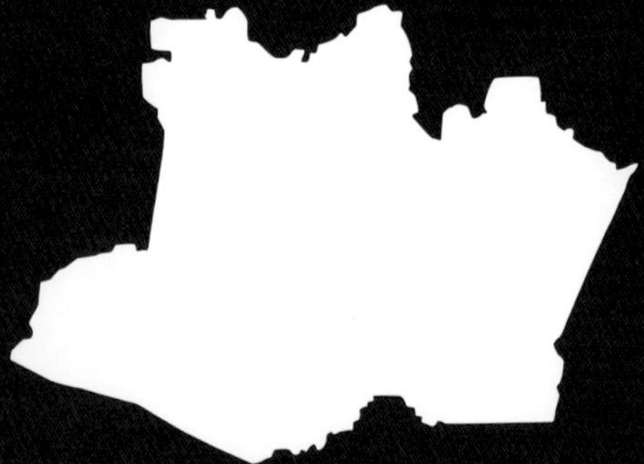

Many macaws are rare. Only **one Spix's macaw** has been seen in nature since 2000.

About **One** quarter of today's medicines were **discovered** in rainforests.

About **80 percent** of the **forests** that orangutans live in have **been cut down.**

One tree makes about **260 pounds of oxygen** each year. (119 kilograms)

Rainforests get at least **70 inches** of **rain** each year. (178 centimeters)

KEY WORDS

Research has shown that as much as 65 percent of all written material published in English is made up of 300 words. These 300 words cannot be taught using pictures or learned by sounding them out. They must be recognized by sight. This book contains 41 common sight words to help young readers improve their reading fluency and comprehension. This book also teaches young readers several important content words, such as proper nouns. These words are paired with pictures to aid in learning and improve understanding.

Page	Sight Words First Appearance
4	are, get, large, of, that
7	as, most, they
8	because, Earth, is, it, makes, much, so, the, to
11	about, and, animals, in, live, plants
12	home, some, world
15	different, for, kinds, many, their
16	found, trees
19	a, cut, down, every, second
20	important, keep, need

Page	Content Words First Appearance
4	forests, rain, rainforests
7	tropical rainforests
8	air, Amazon rainforest, "lungs of the Earth"
12	frogs
15	birds, colors, macaws
16	Asia, orangutans
19	football field

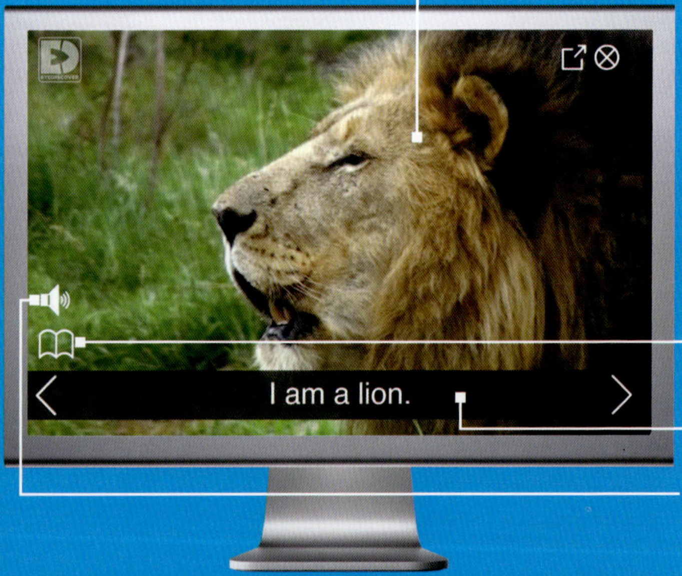

Watch
Video content brings each page to life.

Browse
Thumbnails make navigation simple.

Read
Follow along with text on the screen.

Listen
Hear each page read aloud.

EYEDISCOVER

Go to www.eyediscover.com and enter this book's unique code.

BOOK CODE

AVW42666